Yellowstone National Park Tour Guide Book

By Waypoint Tours®

ISBN: 978-0-578-02083-9

Front Cover - Upper Geyser Basin Riverside Geyser Erupting into the Firehole River

Back Cover - Upper Geyser Basin Morning Glory Pool, Photo by Erika Strom

WAYPOINT TOURS®

Contents

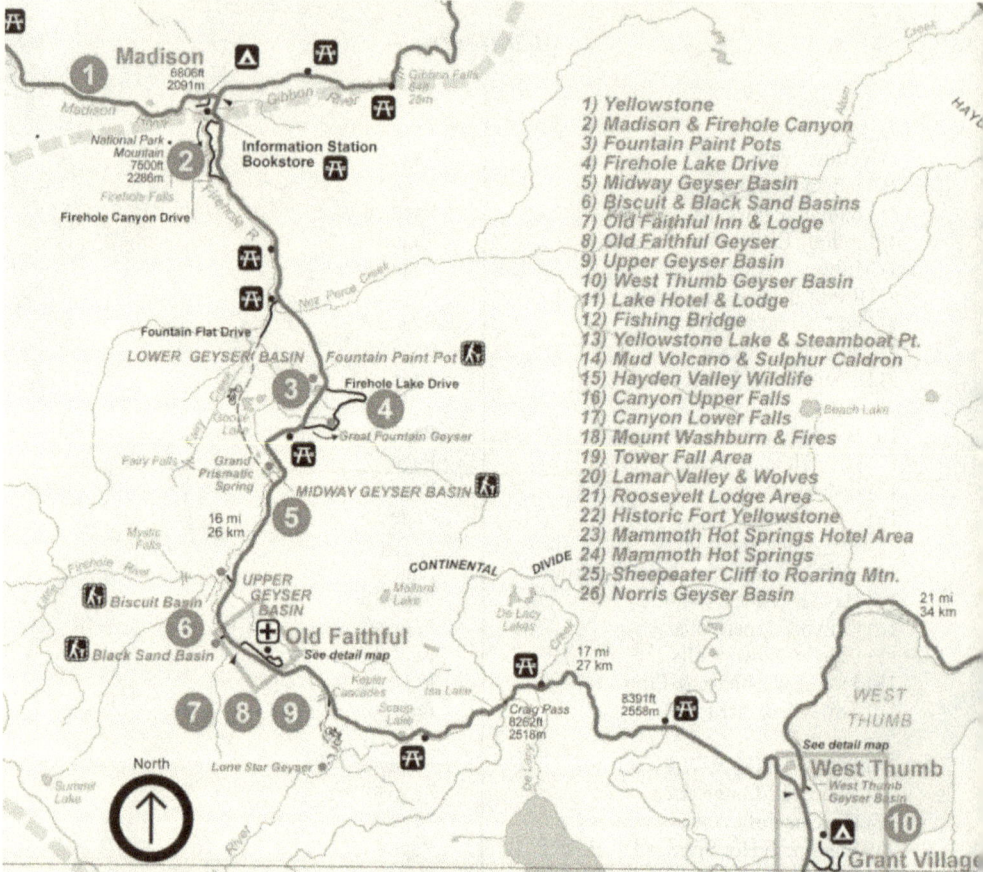

1) Yellowstone
2) Madison & Firehole Canyon
3) Fountain Paint Pots
4) Firehole Lake Drive
5) Midway Geyser Basin
6) Biscuit & Black Sand Basins
7) Old Faithful Inn & Lodge
8) Old Faithful Geyser
9) Upper Geyser Basin
10) West Thumb Geyser Basin
11) Lake Hotel & Lodge
12) Fishing Bridge
13) Yellowstone Lake & Steamboat Pt.
14) Mud Volcano & Sulphur Caldron
15) Hayden Valley Wildlife
16) Canyon Upper Falls
17) Canyon Lower Falls
18) Mount Washburn & Fires
19) Tower Fall Area
20) Lamar Valley & Wolves
21) Roosevelt Lodge Area
22) Historic Fort Yellowstone
23) Mammoth Hot Springs Hotel Area
24) Mammoth Hot Springs
25) Sheepeater Cliff to Roaring Mtn.
26) Norris Geyser Basin

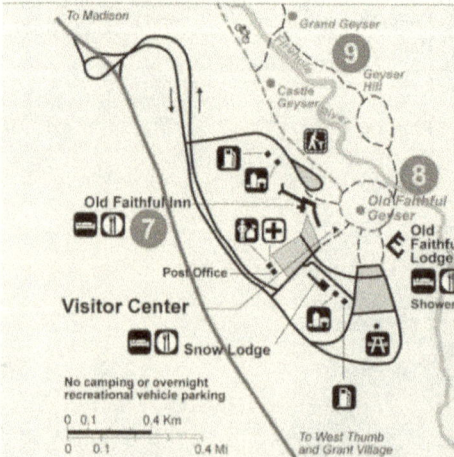

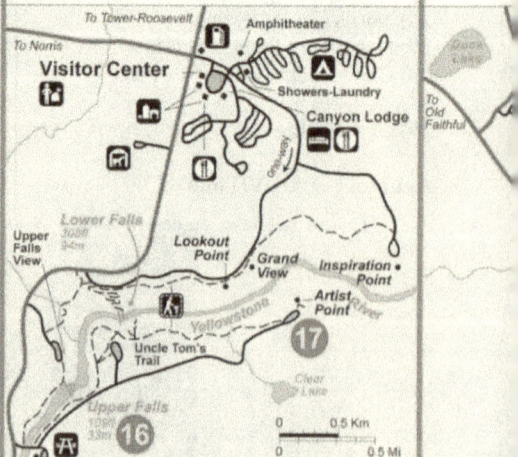

Yellowstone Tour
Southern Loop

Pelican Cone
9643ft
2939m

Pyramid Peak
10497ft
3199m

HAYDEN VALLEY

Sulphur Caldron

Mud Volcano

LeHardys Rapids

See detail map

PELICAN VALLEY

Pelican Creek

Fishing Bridge

Lake Village

Bridge Bay

Indian Pond
Mary Bay

Turbid Lake

Natural Bridge

Stevenson Island

Steamboat Point
Sedge Bay

Lake Butte
8348ft
2544m

27 mi
43 km

Avalanche Peak
10566ft
3221m

21 mi
34 km

YELLOWSTONE LAKE

Lake Elevation
7733ft
2357m

Maximum Depth
430ft
131m

Dot Island

Sylvan Lake

Grizzly Peak
9848ft
3032m

Sylvan Pass
8530ft
2600m

Eleanor Lake

Top Notch Peak
10238ft
3121m

Mount Doane
10656ft
3248m

Mount Langford
10774ft
3284m

Mount Stevenson
10352ft
3155m

umb

Delusion Lake

t Village

YELLOWSTONE NATIONAL PARK

West Thumb and Grant Village 7733ft 2357m

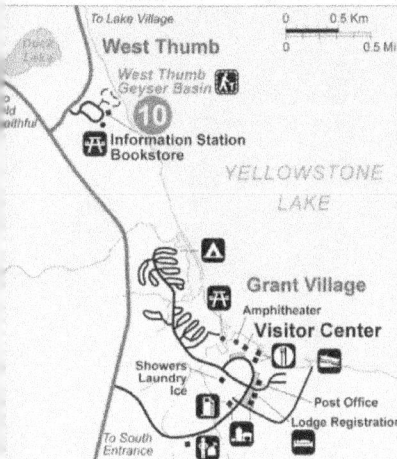

To Lake Village

West Thumb

West Thumb Geyser Basin

0   0.5 Km
0   0.5 Mi

Information Station
Bookstore

YELLOWSTONE LAKE

Grant Village
Amphitheater
Visitor Center

Showers
Laundry
Ice

Post Office
Lodge Registration

To South Entrance

Fishing Bridge, Lake Village and Bridge Bay 7784ft 2373m

To Canyon

Fishing Bridge
Amphitheater

Ice

Visitor Center

Showers
Laundry

To East Entrance

Lake Village
Post Office

Lake Lodge

Amphitheater

Lake Hotel

Fishing Bridge
Recreational Vehicle Park
hard-sided camping units only

Ice Marina

Bridge Bay

Gull Point

YELLOWSTONE LAKE

0   0.5 Km
0   0.5 Mi

To West Thumb

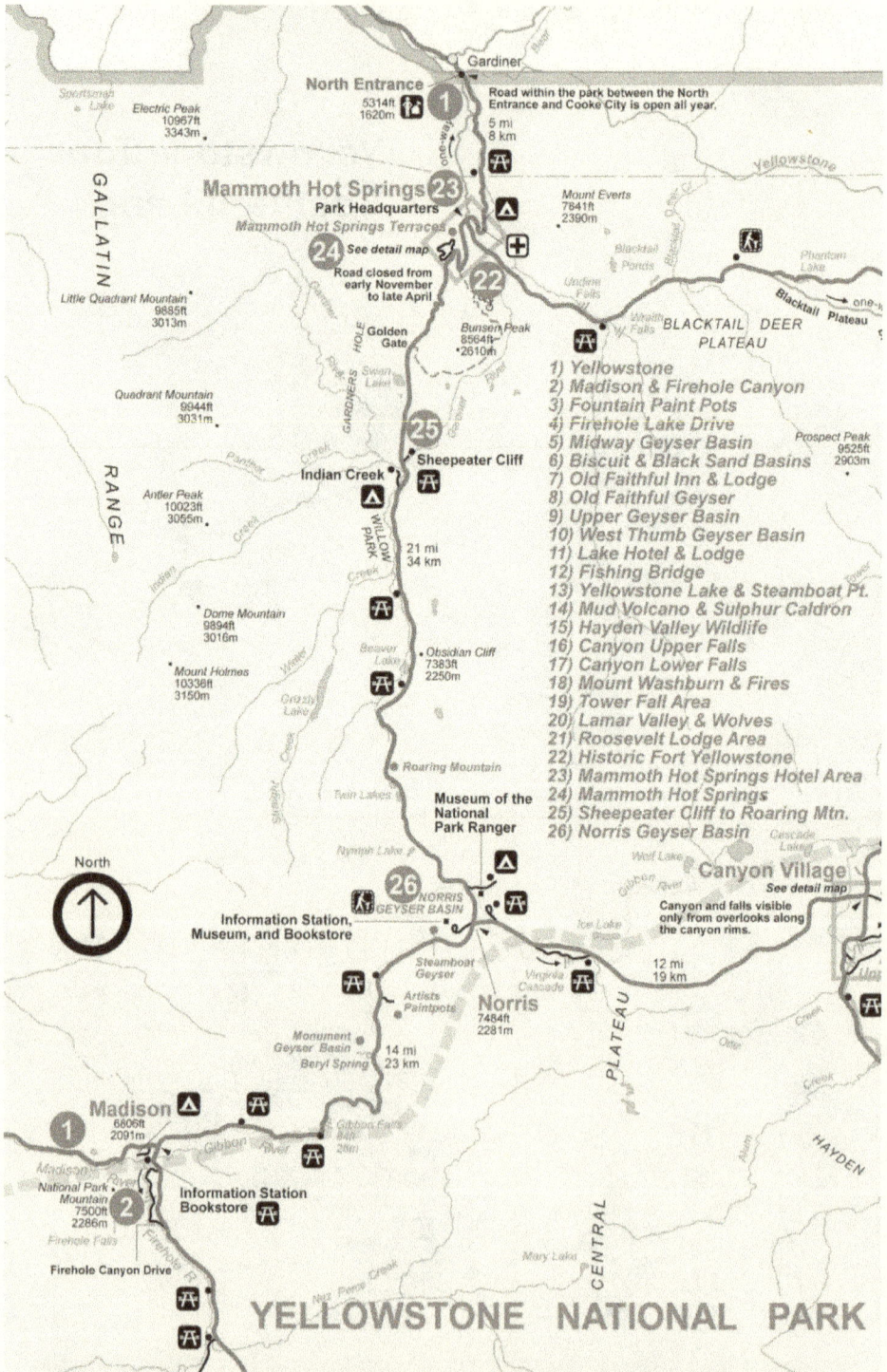

Gardiner

North Entrance
5314ft
1620m

Road within the park between the North Entrance and Cooke City is open all year.

5 mi
8 km

Sportsman Lake

Electric Peak
10967ft
3343m

Mammoth Hot Springs 23
Park Headquarters
Mammoth Hot Springs Terraces

Mount Everts
7841ft
2390m

Blacktail Ponds

Phantom Lake

24 See detail map
Road closed from early November to late April

22

Undine Falls

Wraith Falls

Blacktail Plateau
one-h

BLACKTAIL DEER PLATEAU

Little Quadrant Mountain
9885ft
3013m

GALLATIN

Golden Gate

Bunsen Peak
8564ft
2610m

Quadrant Mountain
9044ft
3031m

25

Sheepeater Cliff

Prospect Peak
9525ft
2903m

Indian Creek

RANGE

Antler Peak
10023ft
3055m

WILLOW PARK

21 mi
34 km

1) Yellowstone
2) Madison & Firehole Canyon
3) Fountain Paint Pots
4) Firehole Lake Drive
5) Midway Geyser Basin
6) Biscuit & Black Sand Basins
7) Old Faithful Inn & Lodge
8) Old Faithful Geyser
9) Upper Geyser Basin
10) West Thumb Geyser Basin
11) Lake Hotel & Lodge
12) Fishing Bridge
13) Yellowstone Lake & Steamboat Pt.
14) Mud Volcano & Sulphur Caldron
15) Hayden Valley Wildlife
16) Canyon Upper Falls
17) Canyon Lower Falls
18) Mount Washburn & Fires
19) Tower Fall Area
20) Lamar Valley & Wolves
21) Roosevelt Lodge Area
22) Historic Fort Yellowstone
23) Mammoth Hot Springs Hotel Area
24) Mammoth Hot Springs
25) Sheepeater Cliff to Roaring Mtn.
26) Norris Geyser Basin

Dome Mountain
9894ft
3016m

Mount Holmes
10336ft
3150m

Beaver Lake

Obsidian Cliff
7383ft
2250m

Grizzly Lake

Roaring Mountain

Twin Lakes

Museum of the National Park Ranger

Nymph Lake

North

Wolf Lake

Canyon Village
See detail map

26
NORRIS GEYSER BASIN

Information Station, Museum, and Bookstore

Ice Lake

Canyon and falls visible only from overlooks along the canyon rims.

12 mi
19 km

Steamboat Geyser

Artists Paintpots

Virginia Cascade

Norris
7484ft
2281m

Monument Geyser Basin

Beryl Spring

14 mi
23 km

PLATEAU

CENTRAL

Madison
6806ft
2091m

1

Gibbon Falls
84ft
26m

Gibbon River

National Park Mountain
7500ft
2286m

2

Information Station Bookstore

Madison River

Firehole R.

Firehole Falls

Firehole Canyon Drive

Nez Perce Creek

Mary Lake

HAYDEN

YELLOWSTONE NATIONAL PARK

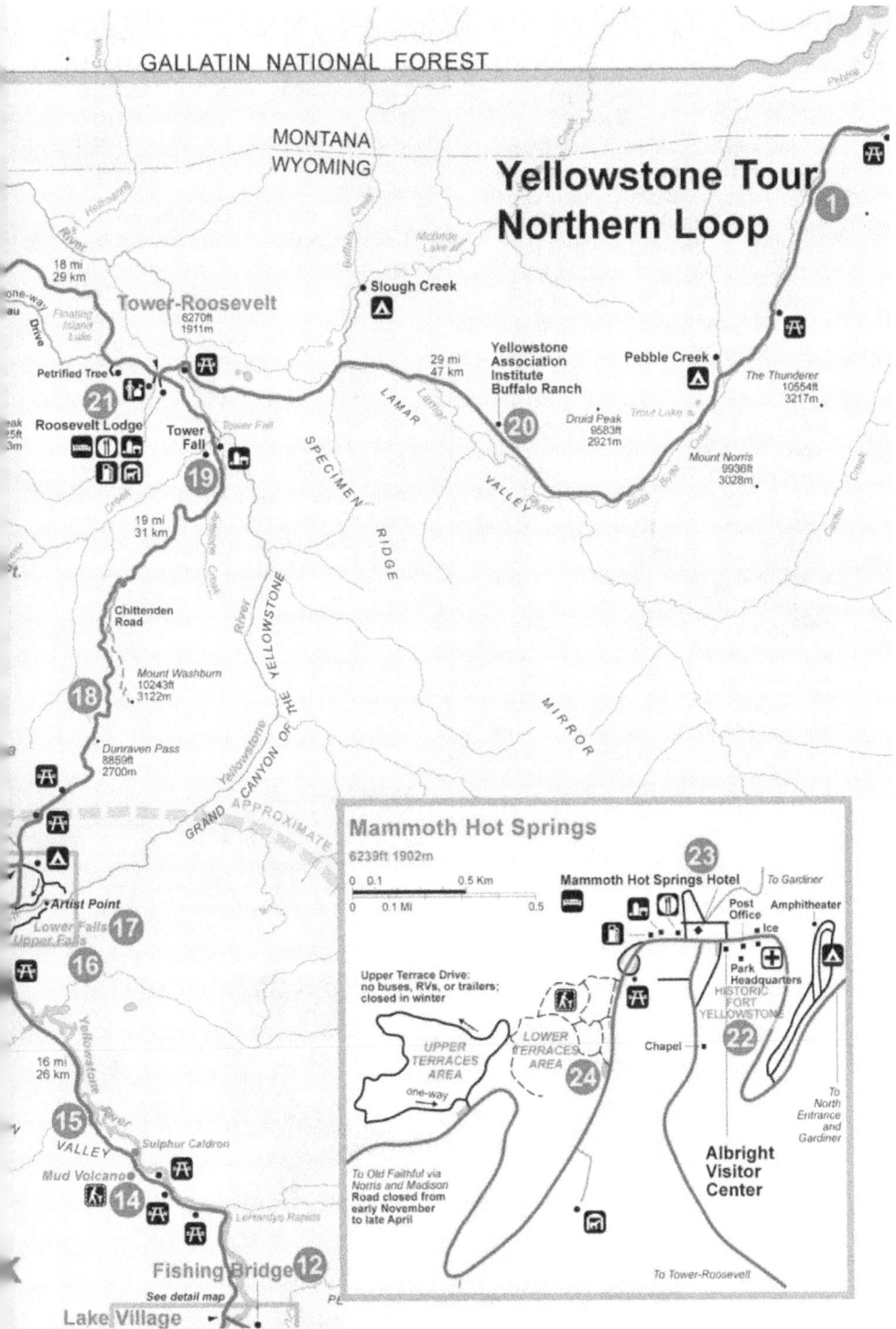

GALLATIN NATIONAL FOREST

MONTANA
WYOMING

Yellowstone Tour
Northern Loop

①

Slough Creek

Tower-Roosevelt
6270ft
1911m

18 mi
29 km

Floating
Island
Lake

one-way
Drive

29 mi
47 km

Yellowstone
Association
Institute
Buffalo Ranch

Pebble Creek •

The Thunderer
10554ft
3217m

Petrified Tree •

Roosevelt Lodge
㉑

Druid Peak
9583ft
2921m

⑳

Trout Lake

Mount Norris
9936ft
3028m

Tower
Fall

Tower Fall

⑲

LAMAR

VALLEY

SPECIMEN RIDGE

19 mi
31 km

Chittenden
Road

Mount Washburn
10243ft
3122m

⑱

MIRROR

Dunraven Pass
8859ft
2700m

YELLOWSTONE RIVER

GRAND CANYON OF THE YELLOWSTONE

APPROXIMATE

Mammoth Hot Springs
6239ft 1902m

0   0.1   0.5 Km
0   0.1 MI   0.5

Mammoth Hot Springs Hotel   To Gardiner

Post
Office   Amphitheater

Ice

Upper Terrace Drive:
no buses, RVs, or trailers;
closed in winter

㉓

Park
Headquarters
HISTORIC
FORT
YELLOWSTONE

㉒

Artist Point

Lower Falls
Upper Falls

⑰

⑯

UPPER
TERRACES
AREA

LOWER
TERRACES
AREA

㉔

Chapel

one-way

To
North
Entrance
and
Gardiner

16 mi
26 km

⑮

VALLEY

Sulphur Caldron

Mud Volcano

⑭

To Old Faithful via
Norris and Madison
Road closed from
early November
to late April

LeHardys Rapids

Albright
Visitor
Center

Fishing Bridge ⑫

See detail map

Lake Village

To Tower-Roosevelt

1) Yellowstone

Welcome to the world's first national park – Yellowstone! The golden rocks, effervescent waters, teeming forests, meadows and streams of Yellowstone have been dually christened by the United Nations as a World Biosphere Reserve and a World Heritage Site. This is North America's Serengeti, where 1,700 kinds of plants sustain 60 mammal and 311 bird species. Here, 150 lakes and 500 streams give birth to mighty rivers and thrive with 24 species of fish. The generally placid flow of these watercourses is spectacularly interrupted by nearly 300 waterfalls.

Like inverted waterfalls, Yellowstone's 300 geysers erupt skyward, flying in the face of the old adage, and arguing instead, that what goes down must *also* come up! Less flashy, but equally intriguing, are the geysers' cousins: hot springs, fumaroles, mud pots and travertine terraces. These geothermal features are variations on the physics of boiling water, are ten thousand in number, comprise half of the planet's total population of geothermal features, and yet are concentrated in the 2.2 million acre square in the upper left corner of Wyoming's map simply labeled: Yellowstone.

Here, tourism became a science. Here, the U.S. Army defeated extinction by protecting the last of the American bison. Here, big government and big business united to preserve something greater than the revenue it generated. Here, preservation became an ethic.

Yellowstone is the example touted to help justify the establishment and protection of 3,600 other national parks in 143 different countries. It's an adventurer's dream, meticulously planned. It's the first and last word of the favorite vacation story. It's where many first fall in love: with the outdoors, with geology, with wildlife, with history, and with photography. It's also where *you* can fall in love with all those same things, for all the same reasons, plus many more. It's the "every-park" for everyone.

Welcome to Yellowstone!

Below - Lewis Lake Reflections
Top Right - Upper Falls from Artist Point
Page 10 - Madison River Sunset &
Undine Falls
Page 11 - Upper Geyser Basin Views of
Grotto Geyser &
Elk Herd near Old Faithful Inn

2) Madison & Firehole Canyon Drive

When entering Yellowstone from Idaho, you will begin your visit where legend has it that it all began. As you drive along the Madison River, where bald eagles soar, elk and mule deer roam, trout await the patient fly fisherman (or the clever river otter), and the rare trumpeter swan-call can sometimes be heard, it's not hard to let your imagination run a bit wild, and dream of what it might have been like in 1870. Could it be here, as Wallace Stegner would later put it, that "the greatest idea America ever had" was first conceived?

Imagine the leadership of the 1870 Washburn Expedition sitting around a campfire along the banks of the Madison River as their multi-month exploration of the region was drawing to a close. Could they not but reflect on the wonders they had seen? How should these politicians and business-men of the Montana Territory best profit from their discoveries? What happened during the Washburn Expe-dition that sparked the movement which less than two years later, on March 1, 1872, lead President Ulysses S. Grant to sign into law Yellowstone as the first national park?

As you ponder the boundary in time where mankind took a major step toward stewardship of our natural resources, you are also traveling to-ward another boundary in time and dimension. Madison Junction lies on the edge of a caldera, the inner cone of an ancient volcano. Although the cal-dera is too massive, eroded, and vegetated to be readily apparent to the casual observer, careful geologic study has revealed its boundaries.

To the northeast, beautiful Gibbon Falls cascades 84 feet over the caldera rim, giving but a hint of the geologic mysteries hidden in Yellow-stone. Similarly, 30-foot Lewis Falls, on the southern entrance road from the Tetons, shows the approximate loca-tion of the caldera's southern border.

When heading south from Madison Junction, depart the busy main road to enjoy the more intimate, one-way, Firehole Canyon Drive, which passes through ancient rhyolitic lava flows. Along the way, you can photograph Firehole Falls, formed along the edge of an old lava flow, or stop for an invigorating dip in the Fire-hole Swimming Hole if open. Be advised, no lifeguards are on duty and the current is stronger than it looks, so swimming is at your own risk.

Tonight, as you gather around the campfire and reflect on the day, what will you and your expedition discuss? Great ideas are possible when inspired by the magic of Yellowstone.

Top Right - Firehole Falls
Bottom Right - Firehole River
Swimming Hole

3) Fountain Paint Pots

When you reach the Lower Geyser Basin, see the Fountain Paint Pots first. Here, you'll get an exciting overview of all four types of geothermal features. Start the half-mile boardwalk loop by comparing Celestine Pool on the left, to Silex Spring, ahead on the right. Like all geothermal features, both are filled by boiling water, rising when groundwater contacts hot rock deep beneath the ground. Springs are constantly overflowing their banks, where pools maintain a better balance between rising water and evaporation. After passing Silex Spring, you'll probably smell the rotten egg aroma of Fountain Paint Pot before you see it.

All thermal features give off hydrogen sulfide gas, but with little water to dilute the gas, mud pots are infamously stinky. Hydrogen sulfide is poisonous, so if you start to feel nauseated, move to where the air is fresher. Although a killer to plants and animals, this gas is food for the heat-tolerant microbes known as thermophiles. They convert the gas into sulfuric acid, which can corrode steel. Here it dissolves rock into clay, making mud pots.

In the spring, this mud is soupy from the influx of rain and melting snow, which allows the gas to easily escape. However, when the mud gets thicker in late summer, the gas can only escape explosively. Watch out, because eruptions can fling globs of mud over the guardrails!

Next are fumaroles, which are the driest of all geothermal features; they give off steam with such force that they roar like giant teakettles or dragons. Red Spouter is both a mud pot and fumarole, depending on the season and the level of the water table.

On the far end of the loop is a group of geysers with eruptions frequent enough to satisfy even the most impatient visitor. Clepsydra, for example, used to erupt every three minutes. Since the Hebgen Lake earthquake of 1959, which registered 7.5 on the Richter Scale, it now erupts almost continuously.

Below - Silex Spring
Top Right - Fountain Paint Pots
Bottom Right - Red Spouter

4) Firehole Lake Drive

Don't be in too big of a hurry to get to Old Faithful. Driving in circles is a good thing … when one of those circles is the Firehole Lake Drive. This two mile, one-way loop ends across the road from the Fountain Paint Pot parking area, but it begins a little farther south as a left turn off the main road.

Most people just slow down as they drive by Firehole Spring; however, you should park the car and get the camera ready. Every few minutes a cluster of bright white bubbles the size of volleyballs surges from the depths of the water. Early explorers saw the rising bubbles as flashes of light from some unquenchable fire below. When the bubbles reach the surface, they splash water two to three feet in the air, making a mini-tsunami that surges over the sinter walls of the outlet.

Surprise Pool is also photogenic, with near-black waters that contrast with its white sinter crust. Sinter, also known as geyserite, forms at a rate of a few millimeters per year, as dissolved silica settles out of cooling hot spring water.

Great Fountain Geyser is a favorite among photographers, almost as beautiful between eruptions as during. Rings of sinter dams create multi-terraced pools that reflect the beauty of the sky. Eruptions average 100 feet in height, but rare "superbursts" exceed 200 feet. Even though eruptions range from seven to twelve hours apart, the bleacher-like seating confirms that Great Fountain eruptions are popular for those who are patient. Check on the dry-erase board for the next estimated eruption and plan accordingly.

Next, you will find White Dome Geyser where you may see a rainbow arched over the massive cone when it produces its 30-foot high eruptions. Not a bad show for what is typically only a half hour wait! Near the end of the loop is Firehole Lake, a huge hot spring, with several small geysers on its banks.

Below - Firehole Spring
Right - Great Fountain Geyser
Page 18 - White Dome Geyser &
Surprise Pool

5) Midway Geyser Basin

Yellowstone's three main concentrations of geysers are named for their relative locations along the Firehole River. Midway Geyser Basin has two of the largest geothermal features in the park. From the road you'll see a steaming waterfall, pouring 5,000 gallons per minute of nearly-boiling water into the Firehole River. To see more, you'll have to approach on foot.

After crossing the bridge, you'll come to Excelsior Geyser, which is now a hot spring. In the 1880s, Excelsior erupted to heights of 50 to 300 feet, creating its huge jagged crater, and so it was thought, also destroying its geyser-conducive plumbing. For a century, the waters of Excelsior-the-spring roiled and churned unassumingly, until September 14, 1985 when Excelsior-the-geyser roared back to life. For 47 hours, back-to-back eruptions suggested the mighty geyser would return, but just as suddenly as it revitalized itself, Excelsior's dormancy resumed, and has remained unbroken for over 20 years.

The boardwalk continues to the *shores* of the Grand Prismatic Spring.

Shores? Isn't that word reserved for lakes or oceans? Perhaps, but at 320 feet in diameter and 120 feet deep, Grand Prismatic Spring is the Pacific Ocean of hot springs.

Through the steam you can see the spring's brilliant colors, which reveal the water's temperature by showing the type of microscopic creatures living in it. In the center of the spring, where the hottest water wells up, the color is blue, being far too hot for any thermophiles to live. Near the cooler edges, yellow cyanobacteria indicate water between 180 and 160 degrees Fahrenheit. In the out-flowing streams, where water is 145 to 130 degrees Fahrenheit, orange and brown are the colors of unicellular life. Because hot water rises, the coolest water, at a mere 120 degrees Fahrenheit, is found near the bottom, and supports the green of photosynthetic life.

Study of the tiny creatures of this "other" world helps geologists understand how life began on Earth and allows NASA astronomers to theorize about the chances of life elsewhere. One Yellowstone species, *Thermus aquaticus,* is used by medicinal and forensic sciences in the sequencing of DNA.

Page 20 - Excelsior
Page 21 - Grand Prismatic Spring

6) Biscuit Basin & Black Sand Basin

Biscuit Basin was named for the Sapphire Pool because it used to be surrounded by biscuit-shaped rocks. However, four days after the 1959 Hebgen Lake earthquake, the Sapphire Pool became a geyser and destroyed all the rock biscuits that hadn't been carried away.

Yellowstone endures an average of 2,000 annual earthquakes. Most go completely unnoticed by park visitors. Nevertheless, infrequent powerful earthquakes can shake the land sufficiently to open and close underground fractures, damaging or rerouting the geothermal plumbing that supplies geysers and their ilk. As a result, many change, some die, and occasionally new geothermal features appear where none existed previously.

Ghost trees are an obvious sign of geothermal fluctuation. When a thermal feature cools down, the lodgepole pine forest begins to approach. When the flow of silica-rich boiling water resurges, the invading trees die from petrification.

Roots draw silica-laden water into the tree. Once inside the tree, the silica hardens into glass, clogging the wood until eventually no water can reach the leaves. Turned to stone from the inside out, these trees won't rot, nor be uprooted by wind, but may stand for hundreds of years if not shaken down in the next big earthquake.

Need a break from the geothermals? Impressive, but more conventional, geology can be enjoyed by hiking one mile from Biscuit Basin to the 70-foot Mystic Falls, or two-and-a-half miles to the 197-foot Fairy Falls.

Farther up the road are more springs and geysers in Black Sand Basin. Don't overlook the fact that the ground is covered with obsidian. Since mankind started making tools, this volcanic glass has been highly prized. Ice-age hunters used it to slay wooly mammoths. Cardiac surgeons prefer it to steel because even the sharpest steel can tear tissue, while obsidian always cuts. In Black Sand Basin, obsidian is not only as common as dirt, it *is* the dirt! Proof, yet again, that the ordinary in Yellowstone would be extraordinary anywhere else.

Below - Biscuit Basin Sapphire Pool
Top Right - Biscuit Basin Black Opal Pool
Bottom Right - Black Sand Basin
Opalescent Pool & Ghost Trees

7) Old Faithful Inn & Lodge

In 1873, one year after Yellowstone was established, Robert Chambers Reamer was born in Oberlin, Ohio. A self-taught architect, Reamer was hired at the age of 29 to build what would become one of the world's most famous hotels, the Old Faithful Inn.

Living up to his middle name, Robert Chambers Reamer's building boasts the ultimate chamber. With a 500-ton, 7-story masonry chimney, and an orchestra pit known as the Crow's Nest hanging from the ceiling, this 92-foot tall lobby is like none other. Even with modern power tools and construction materials, this lobby would be a feat; back in 1904, using only the straight but otherwise modest logs of lodgepole pines, it was astonishing.

Why didn't Reamer use bigger trees? A firm believer in the "working-with-what-you-have" mentality of the "arts and crafts" movement, Reamer maintained, "To be at discord with the landscape would be almost a crime. To try to improve upon it would be an impertinence." Standing among lodgepole pines, his lodge could only be made of lodgepole pine.

Reamer's 50 workers came from the Northern Pacific Railroad and were well practiced at making towering wooden railroad trestles, bridges strong enough to support hundreds of tons of train rumbling across their tops. Yet while trestles only had to be strong and durable, this lobby also had to be beautiful. Reamer added *form* to the interlocking rafters' *function* by decorating balconies, railings, and banisters with lodgepole logs so atypically crooked, burled, knotty, and ugly that they lent beauty to the overall design.

Later in 1923, Daniel Hull and Gilbert Stanley Underwood were not so discerning in designing the nearby Old Faithful Lodge. Instead, they imported massive Douglas fir logs, overcoming the problems of engineering geometry with brute strength. This building was designed to accommodate the influx of automobile tourists, so perhaps it's no accident that the lobby and dining area offer dramatic, "through-the-windshield" -like views of the Old Faithful Geyser's periodic eruptions.

Below - Old Faithful Lodge
Right - Old Faithful Inn

8) Old Faithful Geyser

Named by the Washburn Expedition for its predictability, Old Faithful's eruptions range from 45 to 90 minutes apart. The time between Old Faithful's eruptions are slightly longer than when it was discovered, but the park rangers can still predict them with surprising accuracy. The most powerful eruptions can reach 185 feet, last for five minutes, and discharge 8,000 gallons of water. Old Faithful, though not the tallest or the most powerful, is still the world's most famous geyser. 25,000 people a day see Old Faithful go off, with as many as 5,000 people per eruption.

Geysers are rare; they occur where Earth's molten mantle is near the surface. Usually 20 to 25 miles of crustal rock overlays the mantle. In Yellowstone, the crust might be only three miles thin. Thin crustal rock also has to be fractured deeply enough that ground water can drain down to where the mantle keeps bedrock searing hot. Finally, a fracture needs a constriction point near the surface.

The beginning of the geyser's eruption process is the moment the previous eruption ends. After all the water in a fracture has been blasted out, groundwater surges back down. The first water to arrive at the bottom instantly boils, but before it can escape as steam, cooler water pours in on top. The phenomenal burden of the growing water column increases the pressure and raises the boiling point, keeping most of the water in its liquid state. Slowly, tiny steam bubbles fight their way upwards against the crushing weight of the water.

At a constriction point, the bubbles merge and grow until at last they have enough power to lift the upper portion of the water column up and out, overflowing the geyser's pool or spout. This pressure release allows all the superheated water below to instantly vaporize and the geyser erupts, taking any additional groundwater upward in the blast. When all of the superheated steam is expelled, the process begins again.

Top Right - View from Old Faithful Observation Point

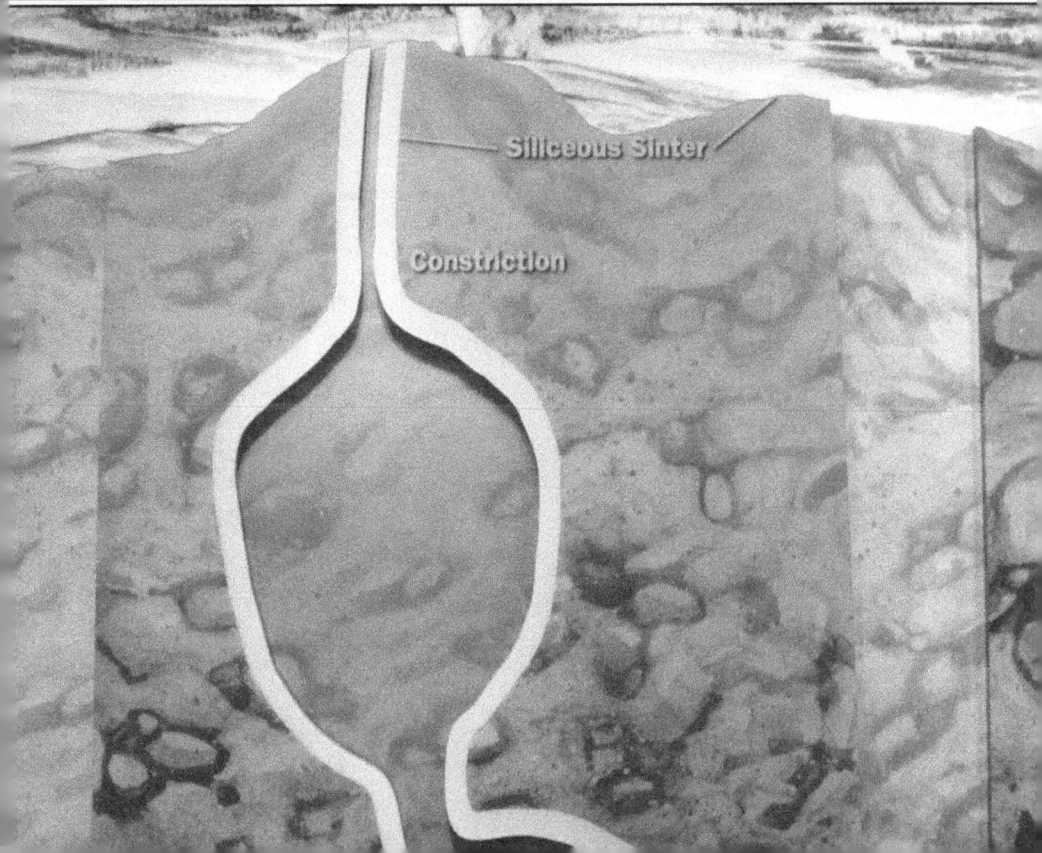

Siliceous Sinter

Constriction

9) Upper Geyser Basin

Old Faithful is just one of 150 geysers within the square mile that is the Upper Geyser Basin. While waiting for Old Faithful to erupt, make the most of your time by stopping in at the Visitor Center and checking on the predicted eruption times of Castle, Grand, Daisy, and Riverside geysers. Plan your path through the basin's network of trails based on the sequence of their predicted eruptions, but be ready for the wonderful surprises of many smaller, but still spectacular geysers along the way. More precise estimates on eruption times may be available from the "geyser gazers." These knowledgeable volunteers are dedicated to studying the geothermal features and can be recognized by their notepads and stopwatches.

Pay heed to all the safety information and stay on the trails and boardwalks. Keep children close and don't let them run on the crowded trails. Over the years, about 20 people have lost their lives to Yellowstone's geothermal features, and dozens more have been seriously injured. Trust that all the pretty pools of water are boiling hot, and do NOT touch!

Castle Geyser sits on the edge of the bicycle path and, though only reaching a height of 75 feet, it is assumed to have been erupting for thousands of years. If eruption height is what you're looking for, nothing is more satisfying than Grand Geyser.

Grand is across the river and downstream from Castle. Being a fountain-type geyser, Grand first fills its pool with boiling water, and then blasts all that liquid 200 feet into the air in one to four short-duration bursts.

Daisy Geyser is perched on a hill west of the bicycle path. The interval between Daisy's angled eruptions varies between 120 and 210 minutes. While waiting for Daisy, visit Punch Bowl Spring. This spring's activity is so unusually calm and consistent that it has carefully and symmetrically deposited sinter, slowly imprisoning itself in an ever-growing circular tower of silica.

Riverside Geyser's eruptions rain down into the Firehole River, and in late afternoon, create a striking rainbow. Riverside is a forgiving geyser. If you are a little late, don't worry. Riverside's eruptions spray 75 feet high, and last for a full 20 minutes.

At the end of the bicycle path is Morning Glory Pool. Bearing colorful likeness to its flower namesake, Morning Glory Pool has also become the poster child for geothermal etiquette. In the early years, many thermal features were ruined to the point of inactivity by people throwing things into them. Though such behavior is now illegal, Morning Glory Pool is still polluted by those who treat it as a receptacle for trash, sticks, rocks, and worst of all, coins.

Hot springs are NOT wishing wells. Indeed, for every coin tossed in, countless millions will wish upon the desecrator the misfortune of being caught in the act and punished. Whose karma could endure so many ill wishes?

Left - Castle Geyser
Top Right - Grand Geyser
Bottom Right - Daisy Geyser

Front Cover - Riverside Geyser
Back Cover - Morning Glory Pool

10) West Thumb Geyser Basin

As you drive from the Old Faithful area toward West Thumb, you will pass through Craig Pass, where the road divides a lily pond in two. This pond is one of a very few strange lakes perched on the Continental Divide. Fed only by melting snow, it has zero inlets, but two outlets. Before you think you've got this one figured out, realize that the water that trickles out of the west end of this pond and over Kepler Cascades, actually wraps around to the Atlantic via the Missouri; while the flow out of the east side heads due south but ends up in the Pacific via the Snake and Columbia Rivers.

West Thumb's thermal region was the first one in Yellowstone to be described in print. Fur trapper Daniel Pott's letter to his brother describing these thermal features was published in the Philadelphia Gazette in 1827. It wasn't until the 1870 Washburn Expedition, however, that a scientific expedition visited West Thumb.

Fishing Cone is the single thermal feature that most fascinated that Expedition and is still West Thumb's "must see" to this day. The Washburn Expedition confirmed the wild claims of mountain men that there was a tiny near-shore geyser-island from which a person could catch a fish in the lake and cook it in the cone's boiling water without unhooking it from the line. Although popular during the early shortsighted years of the park, the practices of fishing and cooking at Fishing Cone were made illegal in an effort to protect both the tourists and the cone.

On the north end of the trail lies the 53 foot deep Abyss Pool. Its rare geyser behavior was first documented in 1987, and again in late 1991 through June 1992. These explosive bursts ranged from 30 to 80 feet in height and occurred several times a day. Since then, Abyss Pool has been quiet. Wouldn't it be exciting if it suddenly thundered back to life when you happened to walk by?

Below - Isa Lake Lily Pads near Craig Pass
Top Right - Fishing Cone
Bottom Right - Abyss Pool

11) Lake Hotel & Lodge

On the north shore of Yellowstone Lake is Yellowstone's oldest standing building - the Lake Hotel. Built between 1889 and 1891, this was, and continues to be, the park's "upscale" overnight accommodations. In 1903, architect Robert Chambers Reamer doubled the facility's size to 210 rooms and gave it a face-lift reminiscent of antebellum architecture. A departure from Reamer's more rustic buildings, the Lake Hotel's white columns and bright yellow walls stand out against the green forest.

This yellow landmark was a welcome sight for jarred and dusty stagecoach travelers of the west shore road, as well as the wealthy who opted to travel from West Thumb by steamship. Though few make the same breathtaking, by-water approach today, pictures taken during sunset and sunrise of the hotel's golden color, framed in wispy pink clouds and skirted by placid sapphire waters, are popular trophies for photographers.

Even if you can't afford to stay in one of the 158 guest rooms, you can't afford NOT to stroll through the spacious lobby and relax in the sitting rooms decorated with hardwood floors, elaborate wildlife art, and white wicker furniture.

Imagine listening to a classical string quartet while gazing through the large windows overlooking the lake, as the summer sun slowly sets and paints the sky, mountains, and lake ripples in pinks and purples.

If you want to catch some really amazing photography, try getting up early and watch the sunrise glinting off the mist rising from the lake. You may even glimpse bison, elk, ducks and other wildlife greeting the new day.

Since the mass production of automobiles democratized America, the budget traveler has been welcome at the nearby Lake Lodge. Built and expanded from 1921 to 1929, this building is a return to the park-a-tecture look Reamer made vogue. Outward-leaning log beams over the entrance form the porte-cochere.

Here, in the early evenings, a timeless tradition is reenacted as road-weary travelers glance up from their maps and guide books for sublime views of the lake and the distant Absaroka Mountains. On the breath of every sigh is the all-too-familiar lament, "So much to see, yet so little time." Don't let the vacation stress of "biting off more than you can chew" sour the experience. Instead, put your feet up and live the moment. Tomorrow's another day in paradise.

Top Right - Lake Hotel
Bottom Right - Lake Lodge

12) Fishing Bridge

The mouth of Yellowstone Lake was first bridged in 1903. To minimize unfortunate auto versus angler encounters, "Fishing Bridge" was rebuilt with its protected walkways in 1937. While making the bridge safer for fishermen, it made the bridge disastrous to the cutthroat trout, named for the red slash beneath their mouths. Here, at the preferred spawning grounds for the native trout, the population was nearly decimated by the throngs of anglers that stood daily elbow-to-ribs along the bridge.

By 1960, park scientists warned a calamity was imminent. Grizzly bears, doubly vexed by the lack of fish and their recent weaning from trash dumps, marauded the nearby campground and Lake Hotel area. Yet, some politicians ignored the science and downplayed the safety risk. Only in 1973, when three out of every five bear-human encounters resulted in injuries in this vicinity and eight bears were euthanized, was the National Park Service allowed to restrict human fishing in the section of river from Fishing Bridge downstream to Lee Hardy Rapids.

"We can't give everyone a fish dinner," said Ron Jones, leader of the U.S. Fish and Wildlife Service's team that helps Yellowstone manage its wildlife. "We want enough fish to furnish food for bears, otters, minks, ospreys, eagles and pelicans. And then, if we think we have a surplus, we'll let people keep fish."

Lake trout is the one exception. The National Park Service would be happy if fishermen would fish this species out of the region. It's estimated that sometime in the early 1970s, lake trout was introduced into Yellowstone Lake and created the invasive population discovered in 1994. This development, and the avoidable but accidental introduction of whirling disease, has been a double whammy for the native cutthroat population and all those dependent animals.

In 2001, all of Yellowstone's native sport fish species became catch-and-release only. While some fishermen are surprised by this and other restrictions against barbed hooks, bait of any kind, and lead weights, the 75,000 anglers who truly appreciate the sport don't hesitate to rise to the challenge each year. Thus, with foresight, Yellowstone can continue to sustain this great natural fishery and its world-renowned reputation for "catch and release" fly-fishing.

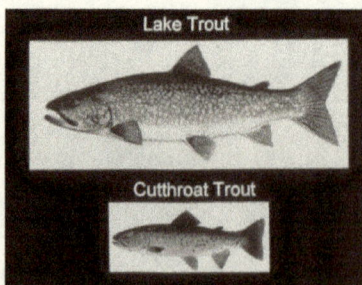

Lake Trout

Cutthroat Trout

13) Yellowstone Lake & Steamboat Point

Yellowstone Lake covers 136 square miles and reaches a depth of 390 feet, making it North America's largest lake above 7,000 feet. This lake fills the bottom of a super-volcano's caldera.

Geologists calculate that in 600,000-year intervals, a series of three horrific volcanic eruptions blasted out enough lava, rock, and ash from the Yellowstone region to fill Arizona's entire Grand Canyon. The smallest, and most recent eruption about 640,000 years ago, left a smoldering crater 30 by 45 miles across. The continual heat from this dormant, but not extinct mega-volcano, still powers the park's 10,000 geothermal features.

The subsequent erosion by rivers and glaciers makes it hard to identify the caldera's rim. Yet, from Lake Butte Overlook, while studying the purple-dotted boundary on your park brochure, you can trace the circumference of this ancient crater. Also, notice the circular boundaries of Mary Bay and West Thumb, which were created as smaller explosion craters later formed within the main caldera.

You won't need a map to locate the crater that formed Indian Pond. The tall, sloping banks of this small adjacent lake make it obvious. The roaring fumaroles at Steamboat Point are another indication that the theorized upward bulge in the Earth's molten mantle that caused all this mayhem still has plenty of life in it.

The whole lake basin itself is unstable. Lake sediments always form flat deposits. However, the layers in Yellowstone Lake slope southward, suggesting that since the time they were deposited, the north end of the basin has been rising. Indeed, between 1923 and 1985, the north shore rose by a documented two-and-a-half feet. Since 1987, the north shore has been *sinking*. Only a restless super-volcano could make an entire lake slosh back and forth!

As you stroll the beaches or boat the waters of this lake, try NOT to dwell on the fact you are at ground zero of a potential re-eruption. Geologists promise there should be plenty of early warning signs many years before any re-eruption. But even if not, where else would you rather spend your last days?

Below Left - Yellowstone Lake Sunset
Below Right - Steamboat Point Fumarole

14) Mud Volcano & Sulfur Caldron

North of Fishing Bridge is one of the most infamous thermal regions of the park. Of all the wild accounts coming from the Yellowstone region during the 1800s, the descriptions of Mud Volcano were the hardest for the outside world to believe.

Explorer Nathaniel P. Langford described "dull thundering booming sounds resembling the reports of distant artillery," and how this 30 foot tall, 30 foot wide cone belched globs of mud high into the surrounding tree tops. Each eruption "shook the ground a distance of 200 hundred yards or more." He was referring to Mud Volcano, which destroyed itself in 1872 and now is a benign remnant of its former monstrous self. Mud Geyser was another star attraction, throwing its black waters 50 feet into the air.

Starting to feel like you arrived at this area of Yellowstone 100 years too late? Don't worry, there's still plenty of geothermal mayhem left, which can be explored using the safety of boardwalks.

One boardwalk traverses Cooking Hillside, where an entire forest suddenly died when the ground temperature soared to 200 degrees F. Another boardwalk gives you access to Churning Caldron. It used to be cool enough to host thermophiles, but since a series of earthquakes in 1978 and 1979, both its temperature and production of dissolved gas have caused this spring to roil water three to five feet high at its center. Mud Geyser may also be on the verge of a comeback if an increase in nearby mud pot activity is any indication.

A little farther up the road on the right is the Sulphur Caldron. With a pH of nearly 1, this pool is as acidic as car battery acid.

Below - Churning Caldron
Top Right - Mud Volcano
Bottom Right - Sulphur Caldron

15) Hayden Valley Wildlife

Hayden Valley is a wildlife mecca. Indeed, as you look down into the wide expanse of this former glacial lake valley, you may see not only cloud shadows, but herds of bison drifting across the verdant green knolls in the summer. If traffic grinds to a halt, assume that a large herd of these 2,000-pound animals is crossing the road. As docile as these lumbering beasts appear, it's wise to stay in your car. Bison kill and injure more tourists than all other Yellowstone animals put together. They can sprint 30 miles per hour and easily dispatch their adversaries by trampling or goring. Keep at least 100 feet from all bison, especially baby bison found nestled in the mountain meadow flowers near a protective parent, or scampering to keep up with their ponderous guardian. You may also see male bison vying for rights to the best mud rolling spot as they try to shed their shaggy winter coats.

Birds and waterfowl also flock to Hayden Valley: ducks, cranes, pelicans, swans, geese, mergansers, teals, ibis, herons and hawks to name a few! In addition to the bison, the meadow grasses attract elk, hares, weasels, gophers, field mice, moles and voles. With this abundance of prey, predators such as coyote and fox are also present.

Hayden Valley is also where park visitors "in the know" hope to see one of the park's grizzly bears. Although population estimates vary around a few hundred, all agree that today's grizzly bear population is healthier than earlier in the park's history. In the park's early years, park rangers allowed the bears to feast at garbage dumps, and then later made a spectacle of it, inviting visitors to attend bear feeding shows. Bears also waited along roadsides for human handouts. All this human-bear interaction led to deaths and injuries among both species.

In the 1960s, a new ethic fought its way through bureaucracy, tradition, and ignorant bliss. The grizzly's ecological role was deemed more important than its entertainment value. In the 1970s, the dumps were closed, trash was exported outside of the park, and rangers did more telling than showing of grizzlies. Visitors still lament "where have the bears gone?" They are now out of the dumps, off the roads and back into the forest and meadows where they can help keep prey species in check, including everything from ground squirrels to bison. Also, the more berries eaten by bears, the more berry seeds they spread across the park for the benefit of next year's host of berry-eating animals, such as birds, chipmunks, squirrels and marmots. Thus, the behavior of today's predator perpetuates the life cycle, and provides a source of food for tomorrow's prey.

16) Upper Falls

The Yellowstone River is the longest "un-dammed" river in the United States. Along its 671-mile length, no segment has greater contrasts than the five-mile stretch between Hayden Valley and the Grand Canyon of the Yellowstone. Like Yellowstone itself, this river has a surprise around every bend.

In Hayden Valley, the river is so broad and placid that American White Pelicans fish it as if it were a lake. Look for these "battleships of the bird world" patrolling the marshes and backwaters, where they nab fish with lighting strikes of their long necks and bills.

A flock of pelicans in flight looks like a rollercoaster in the sky. Flying bill-to-tail, with strong wing beats followed by long gliding periods, they form an undulating chain in the air. Flocks migrating under moonlight occasionally generate a flurry of 9-1-1 calls as UFO enthusiasts report them as being "glowing serpents in the sky."

Any fish or pelican that swims downstream from Hayden Valley will soon be in for the ride of its life. Riffles become rapids, and rapids give way to Upper Falls, a 109-foot plunge into the Grand Canyon of the Yellowstone. Though miniature when compared to its Arizona namesake, the Grand Canyon of the Yellowstone is still an impressive 19 miles long, 1,200 feet deep and 4,000 feet wide.

A short trail from the north side of the canyon leads to the Brink of Upper Falls. Here, 37,000 gallons per second careen around a sharp right hand turn in the river and then plummet over the brink. Standing at this brink is a thrill, but photographers agree that Upper Falls is best photographed from the south side along the South Rim Trail. After you get your Upper Falls pictures, continue to Artist Point at the end of South Rim Drive. Here, you can get dramatic photos of Lower Falls, Upper Fall's big brother.

Top Right - Brink of Upper Falls View
Bottom Right - Upper Falls View from
South Rim Trail

17) Lower Falls

Tallest of all Yellowstone's 300 waterfalls, Lower Falls is a 308-foot drop into the Grand Canyon of the Yellowstone. A mere dwarf to California's Yosemite Falls, and with only one tenth of Niagara's volume, Lower Falls doesn't really have its own superlative. However, it doesn't really need one to be impressive. The colors of the canyon, and even the formation of the falls themselves, can be attributed to the hydrothermal modifications of the rhyolitic rock. Where the hydrothermal activity softened the rock more, the water could erode it more easily, and as a result, the upper and lower falls formed. The chemical alterations caused by the hydrothermal activity and oxidation caused the iron minerals in the rock to become shades of red, pink, orange, and yellow, imprinting a subtle rainbow in the rocks themselves.

Take the short but heavily traveled trail to Artist Point. Here, in 1871, artist Thomas Moran painted the canvas that introduced this majestic view to the outside world; it was the first painting by an American to be hung in the White House. In the 1870s, talk was cheap and writers often exaggerated; so it was that nothing lent more credibility and inspired more support for making Yellowstone a national park than Moran's paintings and the wet-plate photography of William Henry Jackson.

Here, beset by the masses of modern day digital shutterbugs, you'll still find the occasional painter and wide-format photographer. Remember, to them this is hallowed ground. Please give them room to work and respect their concentration.

The "rules of three" distinguish nature photographers from "picture takers." Think of your viewfinder as a three by three grid of nine squares. #1 - Align your subject with one of the grid lines, not in the center square. #2 - Keep the sky in the top row and the foreground in the bottom row. #3 - When photographing something tall, like a waterfall, use vertical format, and position yourself so that the bottom third is below the elevation of your camera. Otherwise, your waterfall won't look vertical, but instead will look as if it's leaning toward or away from you.

How do you get down far enough for the top two-thirds of the waterfall to be above you? Descend one of the three very steep trails. On the south rim, Uncle Tom's Trail puts you close enough to feel the misty spray of the falls and is exactly like descending and then "re-climbing" a 50-story fire escape. On the north rim, Red Rock Trail, also a 500-foot drop, offers the most impressive heads-on view of the Lower Falls. Also on the north rim, the Brink-of-Lower-Falls Trail takes you down to where only a railing protects you from the deadly combination of gravity and water.

Elk, bison, and grizzly bears all frequent the Canyon Village area. Cascade Meadow, between the Lower Falls turn-off and Canyon Village, is a great place to spot the Great Gray Owl, the largest of all owls. Look for their low-flying sorties over this meadow while they hunt for rodents during the evening twilight and early morning hours. Although elk can be seen almost anywhere in the park, this area is the favored summer hangout for "The Boys of Summer": three, sometimes four, of the largest bulls in all of Yellowstone.

18) Mount Washburn & Fires

Driving north from the Canyon Village, you'll climb the flanks of Mt. Washburn, crossing over at Dunraven Pass. If the view from the road doesn't make you feel on top of the world, you can hike higher still to Mt. Washburn's 10,243 foot summit on one of the three mile long trails.

The steeper trail leaves the parking lot at the pass. Being the more forested hike, it offers shade, protection from the wind, and a diversity of wildflowers. Look for Indian paintbrush, larkspur, blue lupine, forget-me-nots, blue bells, and, towering over the rest, the multi-flowered stalks of green gentian.

From both the summit and the road, you'll be able to look down on the extensiveness of the 1988 Yellowstone fires, and their subsequent recovery. During that summer, 25,000 men and women pitted their muscle, training, and ingenuity against the infernos. For months, those fires rampaged without fatigue, burning through a million acres of forest almost as fast as the $120 million thrown in their path. In the end, the fires only succumbed in the way fires of that magnitude always have, and probably always will - to the first snows of September.

Ironically, fighting the fires proved easier than convincing the world that the park was not ruined by their influence. Indeed, every credible scientist and every lay person who truly knows the park can only argue that Yellowstone's plants and animals are better off after the fires. Collectively known as the "phoenix effect," fires increase the production of grasses, flowers like fireweed, shrubs like Woods' rose, and nuts and berries, which increases the populations of plant-eaters, which in turn feeds more predators. In short, a healthier park sprang from the ashes of the old. For a full account of the firefighters' heroism in the face of such futility, and the misunderstandings that still abound regarding fire ecology, visit the Grant Village Visitor Center.

The other, less steep trail to Washburn's summit begins at the end of a winding spur road. Along this approach, you might see Rocky Mountain bighorn sheep, or even grizzly bears. By now, you've read the park's safety precautions regarding bears. Before starting this hike, you should read them again.

19) Tower Fall Area

Tower Fall is Yellowstone's other iconic waterfall. First, walk the road's narrow shoulder across the bridge to view the brink. Here, Tower Creek flows between towers of volcanic tuff, forming S-curves so sharp the creek seems hesitant to throw itself over the 132-foot drop. Now, return to the parking lot and the trail that leads to the more famous views first celebrated by painter Thomas Moran and photographer William Henry Jackson.

The narrow road that continues to Tower-Roosevelt Junction was literally blasted out of the cliff. Drivers, please focus on the road and leave the scenery to your passengers. Park in the pullouts and walk to the railings for the best views of the lower Grand Canyon of the Yellowstone. Look for layers of columnar basalt. As molten lava flows cooled, they hardened, forming individual hexagonal columns. The Yellowstone River's cutting action later revealed older and older flows. Calcite Spring is evidence that not everything in this area has completely cooled.

This canyon is so steep and so deep that here, osprey can fish the river without competition from eagles, pelicans, bears, or human anglers. Like the bald eagle, osprey dive to catch their food, and are well equipped with oily feathers, nostrils which seal out water, translucent eyelids for underwater vision, black eye stripes to minimize water glare, and talons which can turn backward. Turning one of their front talons backwards allows the osprey to turn a fish face forward so that it is a more aerodynamic load, and they are the only raptor which does this. The black and white wings of these powerful hawks deliver a 2-to-1 thrust ratio, which means they can lift a trout twice as heavy as they are from the depths of the canyon. No other bird achieves this ratio, and only the most powerful helicopters can surpass it.

Also, look for bighorn sheep. You may hear them over the roar of the river long before you see them. Listen for the echoing CRACKS as males fight in head-on collisions. A ram's brain floats in an abundance of cerebral fluid. While some might assume this extra water on the brain *causes* such seemingly destructive combat, biologists and crash test dummies would explain that this extra cushioning *enables* macho competition for females. You might also see bighorns on the slopes of Mt. Washburn, or above the road leading to the North Entrance.

Below Left - Tower Creek Above Tower Fall
Bottom Right - Lower Grand Canyon of the
Yellowstone & Columnar Basalt

20) Lamar Valley & Wolves

As you drive into Lamar Valley, look for large boulders and small ponds strewn across the landscape. This is evidence of Yellowstone's glacial days, when 25,000 years ago much of the park was crushed under ice. Even within the last century, Lamar Valley has undergone big changes. Rangers once farmed this broad valley, growing hay to feed bison. In 1902, only 23 bison were left in Yellowstone. Searching far and wide, 21 more were obtained from private ranches. Here in the Lamar Valley, those 44 have become about 4,000.

It's almost as hard to imagine rangers farming and ranching, as it is rangers hunting wolves. However, at the turn of the century when bison teetered on the brink of extinction, the wolf was considered part of the problem. In protecting bison and elk from extinction, a younger National Park Service developed tunnel vision which led to the intentional extirpation of wolves. Rangers killed the last Yellowstone wolf in 1926.

In 1944, Aldo Leopold, the founding father of wildlife management, scientifically advocated the return of wolves to Yellowstone; yet science alone could not undo what had been done.

It wasn't until the 1980s that a new generation of rangers paved the way for wolf reintroduction by carefully fostering within the American public a longing for wolves.

This ecological understanding helped justify the hard fought return of the grey wolf. In 1995 and 1996, 31 Canadian wolves were reintroduced to the park. The homecoming was not universally warm. Ranchers feared wolves would perceive their livestock as being easier targets than the wild prey. Wildlife watchers feared that not only would the wolves be hard to spot, but that their prey would also spend more time in hiding. Instead, the biggest risk is humans, accidentally or illegally, feeding the wolves, causing them to be distracted from their normal prey. As with the bears, take care how you carry and store food, keep your distance from the wolves, and allow the Yellowstone wolves, now numbering around 300, to pursue their natural prey, the elk and bison of Hayden. Hopefully, on this very night, you will hear the sound of success - wolf song in Lamar Valley.

So, perhaps it's fitting that the Buffalo Ranch is now home to the Yellowstone Association Institute. Where bison were once fenced, bred, and fed like cattle, now park ecologists and other experts offer a wide range of classes, while the deer, antelope, wolf and bison are free to roam in Yellowstone.

Below Left - Buffalo Ranch YA Institute

21) Roosevelt Lodge Area

Where pine forest meets sagebrush meadow stands the Roosevelt Lodge, completed in 1920. Over the following decade, 60 guest log cabins were added. The facility has retained not only its rustic atmosphere, it also offers yester-year's dude ranch entertainment. Guests can join guided horseback rides of varying lengths or ride on authentic stagecoaches. After a long day on the trails, guests are welcomed home to cowboy cookouts.

Yellowstone has several entries in the annuals of stagecoach history. On August 24, 1908, a single bandit hijacked a record 15 coaches, collecting over $1,000 in money and jewelry from 85 passengers traveling as a group between West Thumb and Old Faithful. In 1887, a coach carrying Judge John F. Lacey from Iowa was hijacked. The bandit got away with $16 and two rare coins that were Lacey family heirlooms. Lacey never forgot the ordeal.

Later, in 1894, when Field and Stream magazine published an account of how the infamous poacher Ed Howell was merely expelled after a Cavalry sergeant and scout caught him in the act of slaughtering ten of Yellowstone's remaining 40 bison, Lacey took action. Now a powerful U.S. Senator, Lacey sponsored and passed a bill subjecting poachers to two years in prison and a $1,000 fine. The next time Ed Howell showed his face in Yellowstone he became the first person prosecuted under what is now known as the Lacey Act. This legislation is still the most powerful tool park rangers have in combating modern poachers.

West of the Tower-Roosevelt area stands a petrified stump of a once-towering redwood tree. A century ago, three such stone trees stood on this slope, before souvenir hunters illegally removed the other two. Fifty million years ago, an entire rainforest grew here. All the trees were killed by a volcano, but those deeply entombed in ash were immortalized in stone as silica crystallized within their slowly decomposing tissues.

22) Historic Fort Yellowstone

Fort Yellowstone has been guarding the North Entrance of Yellowstone since 1886. Many people, expecting to see stockade walls, drive right by the fort without realizing it. Others tour the Albright Visitor Center without knowing that, while it and the adjoining 30 buildings now comprise the National Park Service Headquarters, they were originally built for 300 U.S. Cavalry soldiers. Take the self-guided tour of the fort, and see how the National Park Service was able to preserve the buildings' historic integrity while making them functional for a modern world. For example, today the stables' "horses" are now under the hoods of the rangers' vehicles. Interestingly, the chapel can still be sought out for spiritual solace, and the "New Guard House" jail built in 1911 still has its original prisoner cells, which can be put to use if needed.

Why was such a large force stationed here? To suppress restless American Indians? Aid pioneers along an overland migration route? Compete in the fur trade? No. Fort Yellowstone's primary function was to protect Yellowstone from invasion by park visitors.

The U.S. Congress naively trusted the private sector to simultaneously profit from and care for the land. While the Northern Pacific Railroad made invaluable improvements to the park's infrastructure, it seldom let resource preservation concerns trump visitor enjoyment. In 1877, the park finally obtained enough federal funding to hire the first park ranger, Harry Yount.

In spite of Yount's dogged determination, poachers slaughtered animals with abandon. Tourists, operating under the euphemism of "souvenir hunting," vandalized whatever they could remove with sledges and axes. Unauthorized concessionaires turned geothermal features into bathhouses and laundries. Hopelessly outnumbered, and with no legal support, Yount resigned in protest. In his resignation letter he wrote, "a small and reliable police force of men … is the most practicable way to see that the game is protected from wanton slaughter, the forest from careless use of fire, and the enforcement of all the other laws." Unfortunately for Yount and Yellowstone, his vision of a National Park Service would not be a reality for nearly four decades. In 1886, the U.S. Cavalry came to the rescue, and guarded America's treasured national park for 32 years until the National Park Service took over.

Below Left - Albright Visitor Center
Below Right - Chapel

23) Mammoth Hot Springs Hotel Area

Beware of the lawn ornaments! These elk are not made of plastic, but 1,000 pounds of live muscle, hooves, and antlers. In the late fall, the lawns of Mammoth are one of the last sources of green vegetation, which attracts elk from all around. Fall is also the elk-mating season, which makes them especially aggressive and dangerous.

Across the street from the Albright Visitor Center is the sagebrush meadow that was the parade ground upon which U.S. Cavalry troops practiced maneuvers. National Hotel guests routinely gathered on the porch to watch the Cavalry conduct these mounted drills. In addition to the usual flanking maneuvers and charges, trick riding and jumping became part of the show. More than practice and entertainment, these demonstrations were a show of force, a reminder that the military was taking their unusual assignment as seriously as if they were guarding Fort Knox.

The north wing of Yellowstone's first lodge, the stately National Hotel built in 1883, is now the core of Mammoth Hot Springs Hotel. In a room off the Mammoth lobby hangs a huge map of the United States made from 16 types of wood from nine countries. It was designed by Robert Reamer, who is most famous for the Old Faithful Inn architecture. Robert Reamer also worked with Captain Hiram H. Chittenden of the U.S. Army Corp of Engineers to design the Roosevelt Arch with its timeless inscription: "For the Benefit and Enjoyment of the People."

No person understood the value of Yellowstone better than President Theodore Roosevelt. In 1903, after laying the cornerstone for the Roosevelt Arch at the northern park entrance near Gardiner, Montana, he simultaneously congratulated and admonished the 4,000 people assembled and the subsequent millions who, while passing underneath, would ponder the arch's inscription. Speaking to them, speaking to us, Roosevelt said:

"I cannot too often repeat that the essential feature of the present management of the Yellowstone Park, as in all similar places, is its essential democracy - it is the preservation of the scenery, of the forests, of the wilderness life, and wilderness game; for the people as a whole ..."

24) Mammoth Hot Springs

Mammoth Hot Springs differs from all other Yellowstone geothermal features not only because of its immense size, but also its chemistry. Most of Yellowstone basement rock is rich in silica, being either solidified ash or rhyolite lava flows. However, here, 20 miles north of the caldera's boundary, the bedrock is predominately limestone. Limestone dissolves in super-heated water much more readily than silica. When limestone supersaturated water cools, it deposits travertine. Where sinter deposits grow only a few millimeters per year, the Mammoth Hot Springs adds new rock to its mountainous bulk every single day.

The upper portion of the hot spring can be viewed from a one-and-one-half mile, one-way driving loop. After turning on to the Upper Terrace Drive, skip the overlook parking lot; in this case, it's better to save the best for last. Continue around the drive to see the colorful Orange Spring Mound and Angel Terrace, where a sudden resurgence in 1985 caused this spring, like a colossal amoeba, to slowly engulf the surrounding forest.

Now on your second lap around Upper Terrace Drive, stop at the overlook and explore the network of boardwalks that crisscross the terraces. Take the trail on the right to see Canary Spring. Alternatively, the left hand trail leads past New Blue Spring to Minerva Terrace, where the ornate layers of travertine look as if a frustrated baker made a landfill of collapsed layer cakes.

At the base of the lower terrace is Liberty Cap and Palette Spring. Fresh limestone drips over the yellow-orange bacterial mats of Palette Spring like the sticky glaze on a massive bundt cake. Palette Spring is so active that the rapid growth of this glacier of stone has closed, and will inevitably bury, a section of the boardwalk.

Amazingly, the outflow from these springs is an underground river that resurfaces between the towns of Mammoth, Wyoming, and Gardiner, Montana near the 45th parallel, halfway between the Equator and the North Pole. It merges with the Gardner River, and only where the two rivers combine is it cooled enough to be enjoyed as a large natural hot tub called Boiling River!

Below Left - Orange Spring Mound
Below Right - Gardner River Boiling River
Top Right - Canary Spring
Bottom Right - Liberty Cap &
Palette Spring

25) Sheepeater Cliff to Roaring Mountain

The road, which climbs up from Mammoth Hot Springs, passes by Rustic Falls, and traverses the Golden Gate Pass, is more bridge than road in places where it literally clings to the sides of the cliffs. To the east is Bunsen Peak, named for a German scientist who studied Iceland's geysers, and who is best known for his invention, the Bunsen burner. Bunsen Peak makes a good home for bighorn sheep, and may therefore account for the tales of the Sheepeaters, a band of Shoshone.

The Sheepeaters not only hunted bighorn sheep for food, but also for their horns. Mountain men reported that Sheepeater bows made from split horns could shoot an arrow "clean through one buffalo and into the next!" Most American Indian groups preferred to go elsewhere during Yellowstone's severe winters, but the Sheepeaters may have been year-round residents, or simply given that title when they were hunting sheep in Yellowstone. They were famous enough to have the impressive Sheepeater Cliff, made up of columnar basalt, named after them. These columnar cracks form when a massive lava flow cools slowly.

Obsidian Cliff provides even more clues to the paths of the Native Americans through Yellowstone. Obsidian forms when silica-rich lava cools very quickly. Here, 180,000 years ago, these specific conditions were met to create veins of the highest quality volcanic glass. Thousands of stone tools found in archeological sites ranging from British Columbia to Ohio, and with age ranges from 11,000 years ago to the 1400s, can be traced back to this exact cliff. The length and permanency of the trade routes required to transport tons of the precious stone across the whole of North America suggests that Yellowstone was as well known to ancient Americans as it is to those of us living today.

Were Native Americans afraid of geysers and fumeroles as some myths claim, or were they as curious then as we are today about what makes Roaring Mountain roar? Were they drawn to the geothermal areas to "shoot" the elk and bison with bow and arrow, as we are drawn today to "shoot" them with our cameras? George Catlin, famous painter of American Indians, invented the concept of a national park in 1832. He always insisted that such places should protect both native beasts and native people. Yet, perhaps it is only today that we begin to realize the true meaning of the phrase "for the benefit and enjoyment of the people".

Below Left - Golden Gate Pass
Below Right - Obsidian Cliff
Top Right - Sheepeater Cliff
Bottom Right - Roaring Mountain

26) Norris Geyser Basin

If you love geothermal features, then Norris Geyser Basin may be your favorite part of Yellowstone. Here, you'll find the world tallest geyser, powerful fumaroles, the most acidic springs, and diverse colorful mosaics of thermophiles. Before descending to the trail system, stop at the small museum for a quick refresher of who's who in the geothermal feature family and some geothermal safety reminders.

Start with the figure-8 shaped Back Basin Loop which is one-and-a-half miles long. As you start south from the museum, hope against the odds that you will be lucky enough to see Steamboat Geyser erupt. Full-blown eruptions of this champion throw water between 300 and 400 feet into the sky and last between three and forty minutes, making it the world's tallest geyser. Unfortunately, Steamboat keeps her own schedule. During some years, she never erupts. At the other extreme, some eruptions are only a few days apart.

You will recognize Porkchop Geyser by a pile of stone slabs that look as if they fell from the sky - which in fact they did, when this little hot spring created a hydrothermal explosion in 1989. Hydrothermal explosions are thought to occur when a closed underground cistern of superheated water suddenly flashes into steam. The water-to-steam expansion ratio is nearly 1 to 1,800 and creates the geologic equivalent of a bomb. Smaller chunks of Porkchop's crust landed 216 feet away.

After returning to the museum, you can continue north into Porcelain Basin on a one-half mile loop. Porcelain Basin is famous for how constantly changing and unpredictable its features are. However, you can always count on the Black Growler Steam Vent. This colossal fumarole is so powerful that its constant blast of steam is eroding a 50-foot long trough in the surrounding hillside. Named for the park's second superintendent, Norris Geyser Basin may remain first and foremost in your Yellowstone memories.

Below - Steamboat Geyser
Top Right - Porkchop Geyser
Bottom Right - Black Growler Steam Vent

27) Norris Park Ranger Museum

When you are in the Norris region, make the Museum of the National Park Ranger one of your stops. This cabin was first built in 1909 as part of the U.S. Cavalry's network of 16 patrol stations, from which soldiers could keep an eye on the park and visitors.

This facility describes the ever-evolving story of one of America's most romantic and prestigious careers, that of the park ranger. It also showcases the living and working accommodations of the early park ranger, which, incidentally, haven't evolved much.

The National Park Service came into being with the 1916 Organic Act, which charged the new service with the mission, "to conserve the scenery and the natural and historical objects and the wild life therein; and to provide for the enjoyment of the same, in such manner and by such means, as will leave them unimpaired for future generations."

At that time, there were already 14 national parks and 21 national monuments, with a sum total of 360,000 annual visitors. Yellowstone was turned over to the National Park Service in 1916, but when reinforcements were needed, the Cavalry returned in 1917. It wasn't until 1918 that rangers were fully ready to fill the shoes of Yellowstone's soldiers, and then only after 21 soldiers, who had fallen in love with the land, were granted transfers from the Calvary to the National Park Service. Without their dedication, who knows what would have remained for us to see today.

Nearby Norris Geyer Basin is a must see, and if you find lava lamps engrossing, you'll also be completely mesmerized by the charming mud-flingers at the Artist Paint Pots.

28) Chief Joseph & The Nez Perce

In 1877, Yellowstone was visited by a very different expedition. Some 800 people moved quickly, traveling from sunrise to well past sunset, because on their heels were hundreds of soldiers. They were the Nez Perce, led by Chief Joseph. Their pursuers were the U.S. Cavalry, led by General Oliver Howard. Just south of the Firehole Canyon Drive is a historical marker that tells the epic of this 1,400-mile exodus.

As saviors of the Lewis & Clark expedition, the Nez Perce were favored by the U.S. Government. However, by the 1860s, the unsanctioned influx of miners and ranchers to northeastern Oregon strained relations even with the Nez Perce. Skirmishes broke out, four whites were killed, and the freedoms of a once proud nation died on the treaty table.

Chief Joseph's band and four other groups opted to flee to Canada instead of residing on the ever-shrinking reservations. Led through the Rocky Mountains by Poker Joe, a Nez Perce scout with French ancestry, these families were able to outrun or outfight General Howard's soldiers for weeks.

While in Yellowstone, Nez Perce raiders commandeered food and supplies from the Radersburg party. One tourist, George Cowan, protested, "I did not care to be starved by a bunch of Indians!" The Nez Perce shot Cowan in the thigh, forehead, and hip. Cowan survived the shooting and escaped by literally crawling across miles of Yellowstone wilderness. Returning to their ransacked camp, Cowan was able to sustain himself on spilled coffee grounds until being rescued days later by General Howard's scouts and field-surgeons. Poker Joe saw to the well-being and eventual release of the rest of the Radersburg party, including Cowan's wife, Emma.

Reinforced by two more Cavalry companies, General Howard's force, now 2,000 strong, trapped and laid siege to the Nez Perce just 40 miles south of the Canadian border. After five days of battle, in a noble surrender motivated by the exhaustion and starvation of the remaining 431 Nez Perce, most of them women and children, Chief Joseph declared, "From where the sun now stands, I will fight no more forever."

29) Grand Teton

Grand Teton is the triumph of national parks. It was the land that everybody wanted for something else, but was instead preserved as a national park for all to enjoy. Most travelers only get a few windshield glances at the majestic mountains as they pass, hurrying through on their way to Yellowstone. The good news is, this means you won't have to share the grandeur of Grand Teton with quite so many others.

First, there is a multitude of wildlife to watch, and while number one on almost everyone's hope-to-see list is a bull moose, that's just the beginning. Bison, elk, and pronghorn can be viewed in the sagebrush meadows along the back roads. Signal Mountain is a good place to look for black bears. 225 miles of trails lead hikers to secluded wonders beyond the reach of roads. Ponds, lakes, and rivers offer canoeing, boating and rafting. Lake trout and native cutthroat trout make these waters all the more exciting to the skilled angler. Eagles, hawks, pelicans, herons, geese, and osprey, among others, ply the skies and the waterways. They are sustained by the land and waters our forebearers had the wisdom to preserve.

Though not as obvious as the landscape, but ever looming in history, is the Tetons' role in defining conservation compromises. Grand Teton National Park is a compromise in every sense of the word. Though most of the park's 310,000 acres are federally owned, Teton also contains over 100 private in-holdings dating back to the late 1800s. Those who settled here called it Jackson Hole.

The park also issues over 700 elk hunting permits each year. Commercial jet airliners roar over the southern portion of the park, making hourly landings and take-offs from a regional airport *inside* the park's boundary. However, if it weren't for these and many other compromises, the natural glory of Grand Teton might never have become a national park and therefore never made available for millions to enjoy.

And last, but certainly not least, there are the mountains - archetypical mountains, they are towering majestic peaks, glacially-carved and snow-adorned; the kind of mountains that all other mountains aspire to be. As the story goes, an unknown, lonely French fur trapper named the mountains - Les Trois Téton. Since he selected three of the grandest peaks for that name, it's doubtful he was reminiscing about any one particular woman.

This is the opening chapter in the always interesting, often ironic, and occasionally amusing story of one of America's most controversial national parks … Grand Teton. Welcome to Grand Teton National Park!

Waypoint Tours®

Plan, Enhance & Cherish
Your Travel Adventures!

This Waypoint Tour® is your
personal tour guide unlocking the
fascinating highlights, history,
geology & nature of
Yellowstone National Park.

Waypoint Tours® are entertaining,
educational, self-guided tours to help
plan your travel adventures,
enhance your travel experience &
cherish your travel memories.

Travel Destinations include:
Bryce Canyon UT
Grand Canyon South Rim AZ
Grand Teton WY
North Rim Grand Canyon AZ
Rocky Mountains CO
San Antonio TX
San Diego CA
San Francisco CA
San Francisco Wharf & Maritime Park
Sedona Red Rock Country AZ
Washington DC
Yellowstone WY
Yosemite CA
Zion UT

Tour Guide Books Plus DVD & MP3s
Tour Road Guides Plus Audio CDs
Tour Guide Books
DVD & CD Complete Tour Packages
DVD Tour Guides
DVD Tour Postcards
MP3 Downloadable Audio Tours

Waypoint Tours® Available at:
www.waypointtours.com
www.amazon.com
www.itunes.com

Highlights, History, Geology,
Nature & More!

Credits

Book by Waypoint Tours®
Editing by Laurie Ann
Photography by Waypoint Tours®
Unless Otherwise Noted
Original Tour Script by Kevin Poe
Maps by the National Park Service

Special thanks to the
Yellowstone Association & the
Yellowstone National Park Service.
Support Yellowstone National Park
with a membership or donation to:

Yellowstone Association
P.O. Box 117
Yellowstone National Park, WY 82190
(307) 344-2293
www.yellowstoneassociation.org

Yellowstone National Park Service
P.O. Box 168
Yellowstone National Park, WY 82190
(307) 344-7381
www.nps.gov/yell

Photo Credits:
Back Cover by Erika Strom
Pages 17, 20TB, 21, 43, 49BR
by Kevin Poe
Pages 12BR, 27B, 34BR, 44, 59TB
by NPS
Page 38BL by Tom Strom
Page 38BR, 48BR thanks to Yellow-
stone Grizzly & Wolf Discovery Ctr.
T=Top, B=Bottom, R=Right, L=Left

Leave No Trace

WAYPOINT TOURS®

Optional Audio CD Contents

Audio CD Driving Tour (78 min)

Optional DVD-ROM Contents

DVD Narrated Tour (50 min)
MP3 Audio Tour (78 min)
PC Multimedia Screensaver
Digital Photo Gallery

Breathtaking Photography,
Professional Narration &
Beautiful Orchestration

DVD Plays Worldwide in
All Regions
Mastered in HD Video in English
* Denotes Waypoints on DVD
PC Multimedia Screensaver &
Digital Photo Gallery Each Contain
100+ High-Resolution Photos

Professional Voicing by
Mark Andrews
Recording by Audiomakers, Inc.
For private non-commercial use only
Detailed info & credits on
DVD-ROM

Optional CD & DVD-ROM Info

Track #) Title

1) Yellowstone*
2) Madison & Firehole Canyon*
3) Fountain Paint Pots*
4) Firehole Lake Drive*
5) Midway Geyser Basin
6) Biscuit Basin & Black Sand Basin
7) Old Faithful Inn & Lodge*
8) Old Faithful Geyser*
9) Upper Geyser Basin*
10) West Thumb Geyser Basin*
11) Lake Hotel & Lodge*
12) Fishing Bridge
13) Yellowstone Lake &
        Steamboat Point
14) Mud Volcano & Sulphur Caldron*
15) Hayden Valley Wildlife
16) Canyon Upper Falls*
17) Canyon Lower Falls
18) Mount Washburn & Fires
19) Tower Fall Area*
20) Lamar Valley & Wolves
21) Roosevelt Lodge Area
22) Historic Fort Yellowstone
23) Mammoth Hot Springs Hotel Area
24) Mammoth Hot Springs*
25) Sheepeater Cliff to
        Roaring Mountain
26) Norris Geyser Basin*

Plus DVD Bonus Music Videos:
Just Geysers*
Just Waterfalls*
Just Wildlife*

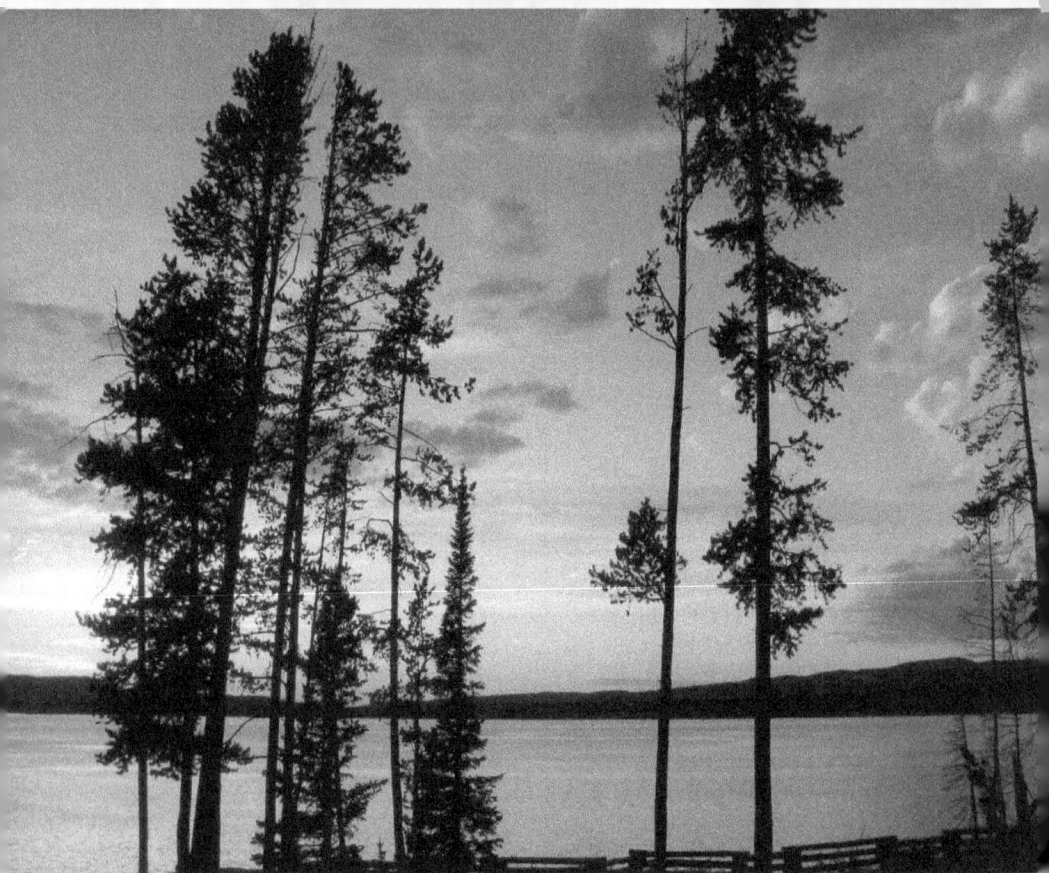

Yellowstone is more than a place. It's an ideal,
an ethic, a love, a way of knowing the world …
Which means it doesn't have to shrink in your rear
view mirror, but instead can grow in your heart and
mind. Indeed, if Yellowstone comes with one condition,
perhaps it's merely that
it should always be cherished … by us,
so that we can perpetually bequeath it … to us.

www.ingramcontent.com/pod-product-compliance
Lightning Source LLC
Chambersburg PA
CBHW031333040426
42443CB00005B/319